First Published
by Redback Publishing

PO Box 357, Frenchs Forest, NSW 2086, Australia

www.redbackpublishing.com
orders@redbackpublishing.com

© Redback Publishing 2023

ISBN 978-1-922322-99-9 HBK

Author: Sally Warren
Editor: Caroline Thomas
Designer: Redback Publishing

Original illustrations:
© Redback Publishing 2023
Originated by Redback Publishing

Printed and bound in Malaysia

Acknowledgements
Abbreviations: l—left, r—right, b—bottom, t—top,
c—centre, m—middle
We would like to thank the following for permission to reproduce photographs:
(Images © Shutterstock) P5tr homydesign/Shutterstock.com, p7tr TZIDO SUN/Shutterstock.com, p7bl Thayne Tuason via Wikimedia, p17mr Will Street Luger Stephenson via facebook.com, p17b Anthony Swartz via facebook.com, p19tr Vava Vladimir Jovanovic/Shutterstock.com, p22 Sergei Bachlakov/Shutterstock.com, p24 Victor Joly / Shutterstock.com, p25tl PopTech via Wikimedia, p25tr Max Heaton - https://internationaldownhillfederation.org, p25br Stig Nygaard via Wikimedia, p26 hurricanehank/Shutterstock.com, p27tl J.A. Dunbar/Shutterstock.com, p27tr hurricanehank/Shutterstock.com, p30t Sergei Bachlakov/Shutterstock.com, p30bl Sergei Bachlakov/Shutterstock.com, p32 Sergei Bachlakov/Shutterstock.com.

A catalogue record for this book is available from the National Library of Australia

CONTENTS

WOW!

EPIC ADVENTURE AWAITS!

WHAT IS DOWNHILL SKATEBOARDING?

Are you ready to push the limits of human risk-taking? Grab your board and let's get our powerslide on!

Imagine speeding down a steep, winding, deserted road at a million miles an hour on a skateboard. Now that'll get the adrenaline pumping through your veins!! Welcome to downhill skateboarding – the ultimate sport for fearless daredevils. Talk about insane!

RISK VERSUS REWARD – IS IT WORTH IT?

Highly skilled riders skate down a steep hill on a longboard at extremely high speeds, risking their lives, addicted to the rush and intensity that comes with this deadly sport. The aim of the game is to achieve the highest possible speed whilst staying in control of your board and your nerves! Some see this pastime as a death wish but others see it as an amazing accomplishment and a glorious love affair with gravity!

THE NEED FOR SPEED!

In 2017, Peter Connolly rode at an astonishing 146.73 km/h breaking the World Record for the fastest skateboard speed achieved in a standing position!

BRIEF HISTORY

Downhill Skateboarding was born out of a need to recreate the magic of surfing, without the actual surf. In 1959, longboards made their first appearance on asphalt roads and pavements and a new sport evolved – riding downhill as fast as humanly possible!

TIMELINE

1959 Longboards made their first appearance in Hawaii as surfers searched for another sport to enjoy when the water was unsurfable.

1970s The Grandfather of Downhill, Tom Sims, fearlessly sped down all kinds of hills on a range of boards. He also designed and built the first longboards and the first snowboard. Epic!

1972 Frank Nasworthy and the Cadillac Wheel Company introduced the urethane longboard wheel, allowing skaters to reach incredible downhill speeds.

1979 The reverse kingpin truck was invented, creating more stability for downhill riders.

1980s Boards designed specifically for downhill skating hit the public market.

1990s The cutout deck was introduced. This allowed the wheels extra room and made hard turns much easier and safer.

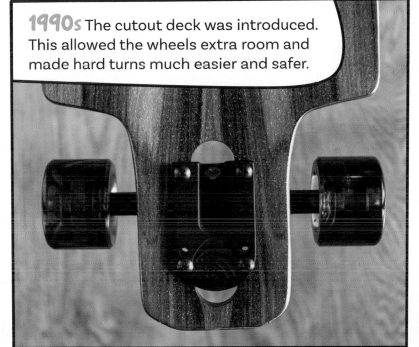

1996 Downhill skating developed as a legitimate sport, with The International Gravity Sports Association (IGSA) as its governing body.

2000 X Games featured downhill skating as one of its events.

WHERE DO PEOPLE SKATE DOWNHILL?

You can't be speeding around in the middle of town looking like a lunatic, so forget urban landscapes and the oceanside! Most places for downhill skating are pretty adventurous, on cool stretches of road, deep in the mountains and out in the fresh air.

Check out some of these dope locations!

SPIN IT!

Skate bearings are small circular devices, made from metal. They fit inside the wheel allowing it to roll. Did you know fidget spinners are made using skateboard bearings?

SOME OF THE SICKEST PLACES TO RIDE!

ALPES-MARITIMES
France

BARCELONA
Spain

TIANMEN MOUNTAIN
China

CALIFORNIA
USA

CAPE TOWN
South Africa

JIUFEN
North Taiwan

LEARNING DOWNHILL SKATING

Practice makes perfect!

Any skater who can ride a flawless line down a mountain has mastered their skills through determination, blood, sweat, tears and plenty of crashes and bruises. So warm up, get your protective gear on and get ready to go fast!

The most important skill in downhill skateboarding is learning how to stop. This is called footbraking. Learning how to footbrake will give you the confidence to pick up speed and push yourself, safe in the knowledge that you can bail out at any time.

FOOTBRAKE

TUCKING

Tucking is the art of making yourself as small as possible to become more aerodynamic. When you make your body small, you create less wind resistance. This allows your body to travel faster and for you to gain maximum speed.

One of the basics of downhill is learning how to navigate an optimal line – through corners and at an insanely ridiculous speed. It is a highly technical art form and staying balanced relies on timing, technique and centrifugal force.

CENTRIFUGAL FORCE

HIGH-SPEED CORNERING

Downhill skating is an adrenaline sport that comes with many risks and rewards. If downhill is too crazy for you, there are plenty of other awesome styles of skateboarding which are all great for a challenge and a whole heap of fun!

TYPES OF SKATEBOARD

Skateboarding has evolved over time with skateboards being re-designed to accommodate the various demands of each style.

Let's take a look at the most popular ones.

MINI-CRUISER

This deck is short and narrow, and easy to carry around or shove in a school backpack. It's popular for entry-level or intermediate riders and is good to cruise around town or hit a park and pull off some basic tricks.

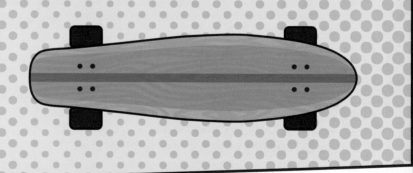

DOUBLE KICK POPSICLE

This is the most popular and widely used deck shape. It's almost symmetrical and features a kick in the tail and nose. It's great for rolling around a park, shredding in a bowl, doing tricks, grinding and getting airborne.

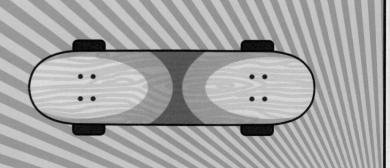

CARVE

Blending characteristics from cruisers and longboards, the carve is designed to mimic surfing on land. The tilt on the board is more aggressive than standard boards, which makes the ride carve on concrete like a surfer in flow.

CLASSIC LONGBOARD

An excellent board for all experience levels and great for long-distance cruisy rides. Easy to balance on, the longboard offers a large riding platform which makes learning fun and laid back.

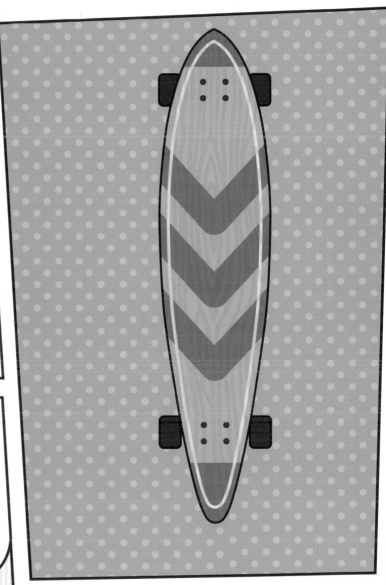

DOWNHILL SKATEBOARD

A downhill skateboard is built to offer stability, control and optimal handling for bombing down hills at top speeds. It features a wide wheelbase and cutaway fenders which provide clearance for the wheels when making sharp turns.

WOW!
Electric skateboards are also super fun and fast!

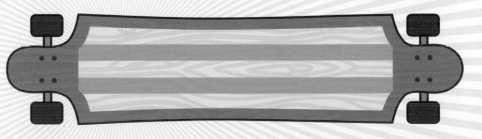

WHAT IS STREET LUGE?

More adrenalin you say?

If you want even more adventure and danger – street luge is hardcore! Street luge is performed on a sled, lying down on your back. Riders attempt to be as aerodynamic as they can to increase their speed, keeping toes pointed and bodies as flat as possible.

SPEED DEMON!

In 2016, Mike McIntyre broke the World Record for the fastest street luge, with a speed of 164.12 km per hour.

STREET LUGE BOARDS

Street luge boards are made out of a variety of materials including wood, aluminium and fibreglass. They have two or three axles that hold up to six wheels - but have NO brakes. Say what!!?! Some boards allow riders to steer with their feet and others just require leaning your body.

POWERED STREET LUGE

If downhill street luge isn't extreme enough, there's always powered street luge. These boards have gas (petrol) or electric motors, so riders can really push the thrill factor!

WHAT ABOUT MOUNTAINBOARDING?

Imagine a cross between skateboarding and snowboarding with a bit of BMXing thrown in. Who wouldn't want to smash down a dirt hill on fat wheels shredding it up?

Mountainboarding, also known as dirtboarding or ATB (All Terrain Boarding), is a mix between skateboarding and snowboarding. Riders can plough down a mountain, making wide carving turns and pulling mind-blowing aerial manoeuvres across all-terrain parks and hillsides.

MOUNTAINBOARDS

Gravity drives the mountainboard, so the steeper the hill, the faster you go. The board itself has bindings to keep your feet firmly gripped in, fat, knobbly wheels and suspension. This allows greater traction and speed. The wheels are like mini mountain bike tyres and are filled with air, unlike skateboard wheels which are solid polyurethane and rotate on bearings.

WON! Mountainboarders have brakes operated by a hand-held lever

COOL STUFF

POWER UP!

Land Kiting is a super fun sport that uses a mountainboard with a power-kite. Riders harness the wind to dirt-surf across grass, dirt or hard-packed sand.

WHAT IS SESSIONING?

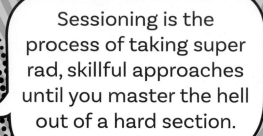

Sessioning is the process of taking super rad, skillful approaches until you master the hell out of a hard section.

When you repeat a particular part of the road or a bend that is specifically challenging over and over, it is called sessioning. It will help you to develop better technique and confidence, so you can ride hard and fast while perfecting your lines.

COOL STUFF

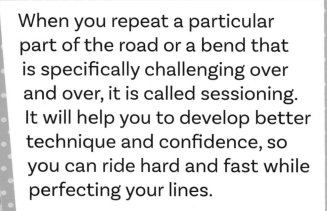

GOOFIN' AROUND!
When skating, you can have a 'regular' or a 'goofy' stance. Goofy, means your left foot is towards the tail of the board and comes from the way the cartoon character stood on a skateboard in his own show.

EPIC!
A powerslide will help you drift around a corner

Getting hurt is unfortunately a large part of the skateboarding experience. To minimise injuries and be a better skater, don't skimp on gear. Apart from the board, here are some of the essentials.

SLIDE GLOVES

Slide gloves are a must if you plan on hitting the hills. These are gloves with a puck attached to the palm. They provide protection for your hands and a way to be able to slow down and control powerslides.

PADS

KNEES

Falling is part of downhill skating, so hip pads, knee pads and elbow pads are essential to absorb the impact and make your falls less painful and abrasive.

ELBOWS

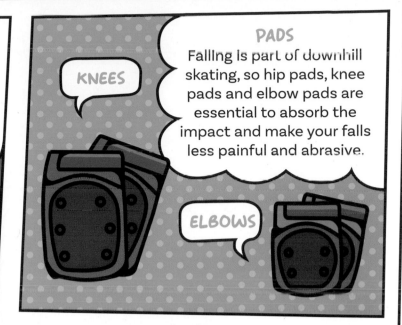

HELMET

A full-face helmet is essential for head protection at top speed. Helmets are ventilated, lightweight and offer maximum durability for high impact stacks.

LEATHER SUIT

Longboard leathers are flexible leather onesies. Leather has excellent abrasion resistance so is perfect for protection when skating very fast at a high level.

LETICIA BUFONI

BORN: 13.04.1993

Leticia Bufoni is a professional street skateboarder from Brazil. She is the official athlete responsible for World Skate, is a six-time X Games gold medallist and has 4.4 million fans across social media.

RODNEY MULLEN

BORN: 17.08.1966

American professional freestyle skater, Rodney Mullen, won his first world skateboarding championship at the age of 14. He has been credited with inventing numerous tricks and has appeared in over 20 skateboarding films.

HARRY CLARKE

BORN: 22.05.1998

Australian born Harry 'Chopstar' Clarke became the International Downhill Federation World Champion after spending 6 years in the International circuit and winning the global series in 2019.

TONY HAWKE

BORN: 12.05.1968

One of the most influential skaters of all time, Tony Hawke is an American born, professional vert skater. He was a pioneer in the sport in its early days and the first to land a 900 – a revolutionary trick involving the completion of two-and-a-half mid-air spins on a skateboard.

INDOOR SKATING

Now, what if it's raining but you have to get a skate in? Well, downhill skating indoors has yet to be invented, but there are lots of indoor skateparks all over the world to keep you buzzing.

HOW DOES IT WORK?

These crazy-fun facilities are built by professional ramp builders, inside big warehouses. There are usually different sized ramps, bowls, street courses and half-pipes constructed with wood.

Some indoor parks even feature a foam pit for testing massive airs and epic aerial manoeuvres. Most indoor skateparks offer lessons, camps and plenty of runs for beginners and pros alike.

COOL STUFF

MEGA!

'The Park' in Victoria, Australia houses the biggest vert ramp in the Southern Hemisphere. It's Australia's only indoor concrete park and features the only indoor mini mega ramp in the country.

There's no doubt that this sport has an extremely high-risk factor, making it viciously dangerous yet wildly addictive.

The best riders are those who get to keep practising, which means being extremely safety conscious. Getting hurt means hanging up the board for a while, so take all the necessary precautions and don't crash and burn.

CRASHING

Take baby steps. Most skaters don't show up on a hill and skate it straight away. They want to minimise the risk of crashing so they can keep skating. Wear protection, warm up, take it chill, learn the corners and work up to the video of hitting it at max speed.

TRAFFIC SENSE

Spotters are people who stand at a corner and signal whether the road is clear. This helps the rider to stay out of the way of traffic. Skaters can also use walkie-talkies to communicate and stay safe on the roads.

DOWNHILL SKATE EVENTS

There are competitions and events held all over the world for downhill skaters to take part in. From the International Downhill World Cup to small events and groups that get together for a weekend roll, there's something for everyone to get their downhill fix.

Some important competitions held include:

WORLD DOWNHILL SKATEBOARDING CHAMPIONSHIP

RED BULL BIG DROP

GLOSSARY

ABRASIVE	damage, wear, or removal of surface material by grinding or rubbing
ADRENALINE	hormone produced by the body to prepare for 'fight or flight'
AERODYNAMIC	allowing air to flow around an object with the least resistance
ASPHALT	mixture of dark bitumen with sand or gravel, used for surfacing roads
AXLES	central shafts that rotate a wheel
BEARINGS	small metal balls that are housed in a casing, used to reduce friction between moving parts of a machine
BINDINGS	device used to hold the toe and heel of a boot and release it automatically in a fall
CENTRIFUGAL FORCE	outward force felt by an object moving in a curved path
DECK	standing area on a skateboard
FENDERS	protective covers that shield wheels from contact with the rider
FIDGET SPINNER	toy with a ball bearing in its centre, designed to spin under pressure
FREESTYLE	flips, tricks and flat ground manoeuvres
GRAVITY	force that acts on objects to pull them towards Earth
HALF-PIPE	large curved structure used in gravity extreme sports such as snowboarding, skateboarding, skiing, BMX, skating and scootering
LONGBOARD	long skateboard, used for cruising, travelling and downhill racing
POLYURETHANE	plastic material that can be formed in any shape or colour
POWER-KITE	large kite designed to offer a strong pull
POWERSLIDES	turning the skateboard sideways while riding so the wheels slow or skid to a stop
STREET LUGE	extreme gravity-powered riding on a street luge board down a paved road or course
URBAN	built-up area as opposed to the countryside
VERT	vertical skateboarding

INDEX